MY FOOD PYRAMID

EAT RIGHT. EXERCISE. HAVE FUN.

DK
DK Publishing

LONDON, NEW YORK, MUNICH, MELBOURNE, and DELHI

Writer and Editor Alisha Niehaus
Designer Karen Shooter
Managing Art Editor Michelle Baxter
Publishing Director Beth Sutinis
Production Ivor Parker
DTP Designer Kathy Farias
Nutrition Consultant Lisa R. Young, PhD, RD
Illustrations Dave Williams from Apple Illustration Agency

First American Edition, 2007
07 08 09 10 11 10 9 8 7 6 5 4 3 2 1
Published in the United States by DK Publishing
375 Hudson Street, New York, New York 10014

DK books are available at special discounts when purchased in bulk
for sales promotions, premiums, fund-raising, or educational use.
For details, contact: DK Publishing Special Markets,
375 Hudson Street, New York, New York 10014, SpecialSales@dk.com

A catalog record for this book is available from the Library of Congress.

ISBN 978-0-7566-2992-2 (Paperback) 978-0-7566-2993-9 (Hardcover)

Color reproduction by Colourscan, Singapore
Printed and bound in China by South China Printing Co., Ltd.

This book is not endorsed by the USDA, and should not be considered a
substitute for a doctor's nutritional advice.

The publisher would like to thank the following for their kind permission to reproduce
their images (a=above; b=bottom/below; c=center; l=left; r=right; t=top):

Anthony Blake Images: 10/row2/r, 10/row3/c, 12/row4/cr; 12/row4/bl. Getty Images:
Bob Stefko 7b; Inga Spence 11b; Tom Hopkins 15tlb; Kevin Horan 9b, 26r/step1;
Eric Anthony Johnson 15br; Justin Pumfrey 12/row3/br; Sam Roberts 31b; altrendo
images 28b; Angela Wyant 14/row4/l; Antonio Mo 26r/step3; John A Rizzo 27bl/step2;
Dennis Gottlieb 14/row 6/l; Renee Comet 14/row 5/c; Ken Usami 29tl; Michael Busselle
27br/step2; Lew Robertson 14/row2/l; Johner 29tc; Marilyn Conway 29bc; Patrick
Molnar 29r; David Aubrey 27br/step1. Jupiter Images: John E. Kelly/FoodPix 17tl,
19l; Pornchai Mittongtare/FoodPix 22r; Lew Robertson/Brand X Pictures 8/row3/l;
Christina Peters/FoodPix 10/row3/r; Ron Chapple/Thinkstock Images 12/row1; David
Bishop/FoodPix 10/row2/l; Susan Kinast/FoodPix 12/row3/r; Rita Maas/FoodPix 17bl,
25tr; Burke/Triolo/Brand X Pictures 17bcl, 19tr; Sang An/FoodPix 18/row3/c; Acme
Food Arts/FoodPix 18/row4/cl; Image Source 19cr; Ericka McConnell/FoodPix 19br;
Rick Souders/FoodPix 27bl/step4; Eisenhut & Mayer/FoodPix 19cb, 20br. PunchStock:
BananaStock 4; Simple Stock Shots 12/row2/r; Stockbyte 14/row3/r; Brand X Pictures
15 tla; Simple Stock Shots 21tc; BlueMoon Stock 18/row2/r; Westend61 27br/step3.

All other images copyright Dorling Kindersley Limited.
For more information, see: www.dk.images.com

Discover more at
www.dk.com

Contents

The Food Pyramid

Eat right. Exercise. Have Fun. Have you ever heard someone say, "You are what you eat?" That's not exactly true, but what you eat *does* influence how you look, how you feel, and—most of all—how much energy you have to run around and play! The Food Pyramid shows you how to make healthy food choices, and every part of the symbol has a special meaning to help you make smart decisions.

Yippee!
The Pyramid helps you choose foods that taste good and make your body smile, too.

Be Physically Active Every Day

The stairs remind you to be active every day—try walking the dog, skateboarding, swimming, or climbing on the jungle gym!

Eat More from Some Food Groups Than Others

The different-sized colored stripes remind you to choose more foods from groups with wider stripes.

I'm Pyramid Pete. Look for my helpful hints about eating right!

Choose Healthier Foods from Each Group

Every food group has food that you should eat more of than others; these healthier foods are at the bottom of the Pyramid, where the stripes are widest.

Every Color Every Day

The colors orange, green, red, yellow, blue, and purple represent the five different food groups, plus oils. Try to eat a food from each group every day!

Foods at the top of the Pyramid contain more added fat and sugar.

Foods at the bottom of the Pyramid are the healthiest and contain the most nutrients.

Grains   Vegetables   Fruits   Oils   Milk   Meat & Beans

Grains

Make Half Your Grains Whole. Foods made from plants such as wheat, rice, oats, cornmeal, and barley are part of the grain group. Grains come in two forms: whole and refined. Whole grains are better for you, since refined grains have had many of their healthiest parts removed. Remember, whole is the way to go!

Eat 6 servings of grains per day.

Careful! Even if a grain food is brown, it may not be whole grain.

Eat less of grains like: cupcakes, danishes, croissants, donuts, cookies, and sweetened cereal.

Eat some of grains like: white rice, white bread, white pasta, bagels, pretzels, and cornflakes.

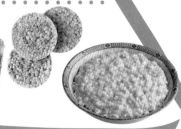

Eat more of grains like: brown rice, whole-wheat bread, whole-wheat pasta, popcorn, rice cakes, and oatmeal.

AT THE MILL

The grain seed is made of three parts: the endosperm, the germ, and the bran.

When wheat is made into white flour, the germ and bran are taken away, leaving only the startchy endosperm. This way, white flour has little taste of its own and is easy to bake with—but it's missing the protein and fiber from the seed's most nutritious parts!

The Wheat Harvest
Most flour comes from wheat, which grows in fields like this one.

TOO WHITE TO BE TRUE

White flour is bleached to its pure color with the same chemicals used to bleach clothes!

Vegetables

Vary Your Veggies.
A vegetable's color tells you what it can do for your body. Dark green vegetables help with strong bones and teeth, while bright orange veggies help your eyes stay strong and your body fight disease. Try to eat a rainbow of vegetables— raw, cooked, fresh, or frozen, they're all part of this group!

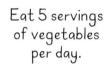

Eat 5 servings of vegetables per day.

Salad can be healthy or not—it all depends on the dressing!

Eat less of veggies like: onion rings, french fries, buttery mashed potatoes, and creamed spinach.

Eat some of veggies like: corn on the cob, canned veggies, lettuce with dressing, and sweet potatoes.

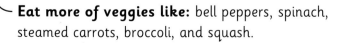

Eat more of veggies like: bell peppers, spinach, steamed carrots, broccoli, and squash.

COLOR POWER!

A substance called beta-carotene gives carrots (and most orange veggies) their color. Beta-carotene is important for healthy eyesight.

Out of the Ground
Carrots on big farms are harvested with machines like this one.

FRUIT OR VEGETABLE?

Scientifically, any plant that contains seeds is a fruit—which makes tomatoes, peppers, and cucumbers all fruits! Still, we tend to call any plant we eat with our main meal a vegetable.

Legally, the tomato *is* a vegetable: an 1893 U.S. Supreme Court decision declared it so for tax purposes!

Fruits

Many juices contain very little fruit. Look for 100% fruit juice!

Focus on Fruits.

Delicious fruit can be a snack, a dessert, or a healthy addition to cereal, yogurt, or even ice cream. Just like vegetables, fruits contain different vitamins and minerals depending on their color. So whether they're canned, dried, whole, or in a juice, vary the color when you choose your fruits!

Eat 3 servings of fruits per day.

Eat less of fruits like: sugared jam and preserves, chocolate-covered raisins, banana chips, apple pie, and candied apples.

FRUIT IN LIGHT SYRUP

Eat some of fruits like: applesauce, canned fruit in light syrup, and dried fruit.

Eat more of fruits like: tangerines, peaches, bananas, strawberries, pears, apples, and blueberries.

10

FRUITS OF THE WORLD

Many fruits come from North America, but tropical fruits like pineapples and bananas must be flown in from the tropics!

The freshest, best-tasting fruit is usually grown in your local area.

In Groves They Grow

Oranges and other citrus fruits grow on trees in warm-weather climates.

DON'T FORGET YOUR FIBER

One medium apple has 3 grams of fiber, but one cup of apple juice has almost none!

Milk

Get Your Calcium-Rich Foods! Milk products are important because they supply calcium and protein, which your body needs to make strong teeth and bones and to help you grow. It's important to choose carefully, however, because many dairy products contain a lot of fat. Look for low- and fat-free foods in this group.

Soy milk is good for you, but contains less calcium than cow's milk.

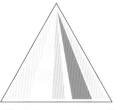

Eat 3 servings of milk per day.

Eat less of milk foods like: milk shakes, whole-fat chocolate milk, and whole-fat ice cream.

WHOLE-FAT CHOCOLATE MILK

Eat some of milk foods like: American cheese and other cheeses, fruit-flavored yogurt, and frozen yogurt.

FAT-FREE MILK

Eat more of milk foods like: plain low-fat yogurt, fat-free milk, low-fat string cheese, and cottage cheese.

MILK FACTS

- It takes 21 pounds of milk to make one pound of butter.
- Milk cools down your mouth after you eat spicy foods much more effectively than water or juice.
- About one-fifth of the cheese produced in the U.S. is used on pizzas.

Mooooooo! Most milk we drink comes from cows, but some people drink milk from goats or sheep, too.

NO MILK? Some people are "lactose intolerant," which means their bodies have a hard time digesting dairy products.

Meat & Beans

Go Lean with Protein.

Red meat, chicken, fish, beans, eggs, nuts, and seeds are all part of this group. Meat and beans provide protein to fuel your body, but make sure to choose lean or low-fat options!

Eat 5 ounces of meat and beans per day.

Grilling and baking are healthy ways to cook meat!

Eat less of proteins like: hamburgers, chicken nuggets, salami, pepperoni, bacon, and deep-fried fish sticks.

Eat some of proteins like: chicken with its skin, eggs, peanut butter, and grilled steaks.

Eat more of proteins like: skinless chicken breast, beans, grilled or canned fish, and turkey.

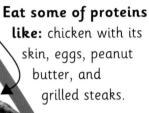

Vegetarian Options

For people who don't eat meat, there are healthy and not-so-healthy choices. For instance, nuts contain more fat than beans, and deep-fried foods are full of fat as well.

Less of:
Falafel

Some of:
Nuts

More of:
Tofu

BALONEY!

A baloney, salami, or pepperoni sandwich can be delicious, but try to limit processed meats in your diet.

Fresh chicken or turkey has less salt, less fat, and just as many nutrients to fuel your body at lunchtime!

Sprouting Beans
When dry beans get water, they sprout. Sprouted beans have even MORE nutrients than dried ones!

Juicy Steak
It's a butcher's job to cut enormous pieces of cow into the steaks we recognize.

MAGIC BEANS
Even though beans are vegetables, they have so much protein that they count as meat in your diet! Beans are also low in fat and high in fiber.

Mixed Dishes

Create a Healthy Combo! A mixed dish is one that contains foods from different food groups. For example, spaghetti has pasta from the grain group, tomatoes from the vegetable group, and sometimes even cheese from the milk group! How can you make your favorite mixed dishes healthy?

What if your hamburger were on a whole-wheat bun?

Eat less of mixed dishes like: cheeseburgers, chocolate chip cookies, and macaroni and cheese.

Eat some of mixed dishes like: spaghetti marinara, chicken noodle soup, and vegetable pizza.

Eat more of mixed dishes like: minestrone soup, PB&J on whole-wheat bread, fruit with yogurt, and salmon sushi.

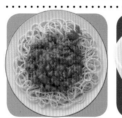  

How's It Prepared?

Often, whether a food is healthy depends on how it was prepared. Was it **deep-fried?** Was it **baked** or **roasted**? Or was it simply **steamed** or **boiled?** Chicken

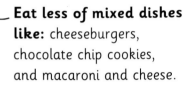

stir-fry, sautéed with a small amount of oil, is much healthier than fried chicken. The less fat in the cooking process, the less fat ends up in your food!

What's In a Noodle?
Did you know that instant ramen noodles are fried before they're packaged? Try making veggie ramen with spaghetti or udon noodles instead!

PICK YOUR PIZZA WISELY!
Pizza, like most mixed foods, can be great for you, so-so for you, or just plain unhealthy! What's on *your* pizza?

Eat less of pizzas like: pepperoni, sausage, bacon, and extra cheese.

Eat some of pizzas like: plain cheese, and Canadian bacon on white crust.

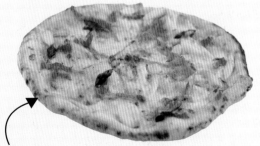

Eat more of pizzas like: veggie or low-fat mozzarella on whole-wheat crust.

In a Day...

What Makes a Healthy Day's Menu?

A growing nine-year-old should eat 1,800 calories per day, spread out among the five food groups and including some healthy oils.

> You may need more or less calories, depending on how active you are!

Callum is nine years old. He's physically active sometimes. Each day, he needs to eat:

Grains: 6 servings
Vegetables: 5 servings
Fruits: 3 servings
Milk: 3 servings
Meat & Beans: 5 ounces

Check it Out!

This table holds a healthy day's diet for Callum. Which foods has he chosen from each group?

Create Your Own!

These examples can help you create your day's healthy menu. Most examples equal one serving. Use them to get an idea of portion size, so you can determine one serving of your favorite foods!

Grains
1 cup whole-grain boxed breakfast cereal
1 slice whole-wheat toast
1 hamburger bun (2 servings)
$1/2$ cup cooked brown rice
$1/2$ cup cooked pasta
1 slice white bread
3 cups lowfat popcorn

Vegetables
1 small baked sweet potato
6 baby carrots
1 large ear of corn
1 medium baked potato
1 cup cooked greens
3 spears broccoli
1 cup chopped lettuce

HOW MUCH TO EAT?

Often, we eat more than we should because we don't pay attention to portion size! Consider the examples below when you're deciding how much food to eat.

3 ounces of meat is the size of a deck of cards.

1 cup of pasta or veggies is the size of a baseball.

Fruits

1 small apple or 1/2 large apple
1 large orange
1 snack-sized container of peaches
1 small watermelon wedge
1/3 cup 100% orange juice
1 small box raisins
1 large plum

Milk

1 snack-sized low-fat or fat-free yogurt
2 ounces low-fat or fat-free American cheese
1 1/2 ounces low-fat or fat-free cheddar cheese
1 1/2 cups light ice cream
1 cup fat-free milk

Meat & Beans

1/4 cup cooked beans or tofu
1 small chicken breast half (3 ounces)
1 small lean hamburger (3 ounces)
1 tablespoon peanut butter
1 slice of turkey
1 hard-boiled egg
1/2 ounce of nuts

Food Labels

Learn the Label. Most foods come with a handy nutrition label to help you figure out what's in what you're eating. Look below to learn each section's meaning for your body, and soon you'll be a label-reading superstar!

Serving Size lets you know how much of this food is equal to one serving.

Servings Per Container can help you judge portion size. If there are two servings, half the can is one serving!

% Daily Value tells you what part of your daily needs this food provides. This is very important when considering how your diet fits together!

This section covers key **vitamins and minerals.**

Calories are units of energy used to fuel your body.

Total Fat gives you the total amount of all types of fat found in one serving of this food.

Sodium is salt. You don't want to eat too much!

Protein and carbohydrates are important sources of calories.

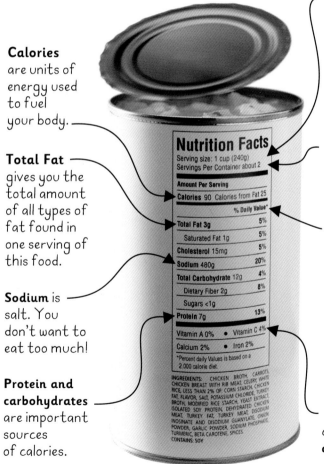

Nutrition Facts

Serving size: 1 cup (240g)
Servings Per Container about 2

Amount Per Serving

Calories 90 Calories from Fat 25

% Daily Value*

Total Fat 3g — 5%

Saturated Fat 1g — 5%

Cholesterol 15mg — 5%

Sodium 480g — 20%

Total Carbohydrate 12g — 4%

Dietary Fiber 2g — 8%

Sugars <1g

Protein 7g — 13%

Vitamin A 0% • Vitamin C 4%

Calcium 2% • Iron 2%

*Percent daily Values is based on a 2,000 calorie diet.

INGREDIENTS: CHICKEN BROTH, CARROTS, CHICKEN BREAST WITH RIB MEAT, CELERY, WHITE RICE, LESS THAN 2% OF: CORN STARCH, CHICKEN FAT, FLAVOR, SALT, POTASSIUM CHLORIDE, TURKEY BROTH, MODIFIED RICE STARCH, YEAST EXTRACT, ISOLATED SOY PROTEIN, DEHYDRATED CHICKEN MEAT, TURKEY FAT, TURKEY MEAT, DISODIUM INOSINATE AND DISODIUM GUANYLATE, ONION POWDER, GARLIC POWDER, SODIUM PHOSPHATE, TURMERIC, BETA CAROTENE, SPICES
CONTAINS: SOY

Play the Label Game!

Here are three labels from different containers of milk. One is from whole milk, one is from low-fat milk, and one is from fat-free milk. Can you tell which is which?

Most milk products come in whole-fat and lower-fat varieties!

1

Nutrition Facts
Serving Size 8 fl oz (245g)
Servings Per Container 8

Amount Per Serving

Calories 130	Calories from Fat 45	
		%Daily Value*
Total Fat 5g		**8 %**
Saturated Fat 3g		**15 %**
Trans Fat 0g		**0 %**
Cholesterol 20mg		**7 %**
Sodium 125mg		**5 %**
Total Carbohydrate 13g		**4 %**
Dietary Fiber 0g		**0 %**
Sugars 12g		
Protein 8g		

Vitamin A 10%	•	Vitamin C 4%
Calcium 30%	•	Iron 0%

* Percent Daily Values are based on a 2,000 calorie diet.

2

Nutrition Facts
Serving Size 8 fl oz (245g)
Servings Per Container 8

Amount Per Serving

Calories 150	Calories from Fat 70	
		%Daily Value*
Total Fat 8g		**12 %**
Saturated Fat 5g		**25 %**
Trans Fat 0g		**0 %**
Cholesterol 35mg		**11 %**
Sodium 125mg		**5 %**
Total Carbohydrate 12g		**4 %**
Dietary Fiber 0g		**0 %**
Sugars 12g		
Protein 8g		

Vitamin A 6%	•	Vitamin C 4%
Calcium 30%	•	Iron 0%

* Percent Daily Values are based on a 2,000 calorie diet.

3

Nutrition Facts
Serving Size 8 fl oz (245g)
Servings Per Container 8

Amount Per Serving

Calories 90	Calories from Fat 0	
		%Daily Value*
Total Fat 0g		**0 %**
Saturated Fat 0g		**0 %**
Trans Fat 0g		**0 %**
Cholesterol < 5mg		**0 %**
Sodium 130mg		**5 %**
Total Carbohydrate 12g		**4 %**
Dietary Fiber 0g		**0 %**
Sugars 12g		
Protein 8g		

Vitamin A 10%	•	Vitamin C 4%
Calcium 30%	•	Iron 0%

* Percent Daily Values are based on a 2,000 calorie diet.

ANSWERS: 1 = Low-Fat Milk 2 = Whole Milk 3 = Fat-Free Milk

Making Choices

All in Moderation

Life wouldn't be any fun without cake, would it?

One slice of cake is just fine.

Being healthy doesn't mean not eating cake—it just means considering *how much*.

One whole cake is too much!

It's All About Choices. Now that you know how much food you should eat and which food groups it should come from, how can you use that knowledge as you go about your day? Check out these handy tips to make the power of the Pyramid work for you.

POPULAR FAST FOODS	TOTAL FAT (grams)
Hamburger	9
Quarter-pound hamburger	18
Fried-fish-filet sandwich	18
Crispy fried chicken	23
Chicken nuggets (10 pieces)	24
Beef soft taco, without cheese	8
Beef taco, regular style, without cheese	7
Bean burrito, no cheese	8
Taco salad with ground beef, no cheese	39

Fast Food Doesn't Have to Be Bad

Food: It all depends on which items you choose. Look at the chart above to discover how much fat is in your favorite fast foods. Next time, try the beef soft taco instead of the chicken nuggets!

What do you think makes fried chicken less healthy than a small hamburger?

So Much to Think About! Every time you eat something, you're making a choice about how you'll feel and how well your body will work. Below, you'll find some advice on how to deal with some common choices.

HOMEMADE vs. PROCESSED

A homemade cookie is generally much healthier than one from a package, especially if it contains whole grains like oatmeal!

Many packaged cookies contain trans fats and other preservatives that are difficult for your body to process.

RAW vs. COOKED

A raw carrot contains twice the vitamins of a cooked one. The same is true for many veggies!

Heat breaks down the nutrients in a vegetable—but as long as you don't add too much fat while cooking, it's still great for you!

ORGANIC vs. NON-ORGANIC

Organic vegetables are grown without pesticides or other potentially unhealthy chemicals.

Organic vegetables can be expensive. If you eat non-organic produce, be sure to wash it to remove wax or chemicals.

NATURAL vs. SUGAR-COATED

A whole-grain breakfast like cooked oatmeal is healthier than cereal coated in sugar or other sweeteners.

Not all boxed cereals contain added sugar. Be sure to use your knowledge of labels to check what's going into your bowl!

Food Paths

How Do Familiar Foods End Up on Your Table?

We've followed one food from each group on its journey from the farm to your plate. Are there steps in these paths you've never considered? When you think about where your food comes from, you'll pay attention to what you eat—and that's the number-one secret to a healthy diet!

Wow! There's a lot of work that happens before snack time!

SANDWICH BREAD

1 Wheat stalks grow in large fields.

2 Combines and tractors harvest the wheat.

3 The wheat is ground into flour.

4 The bakery makes flour into bread for sandwiches.

CARROT STICKS

1 Machines pull fully grown carrots from the ground.

2 The carrot harvest is taken to a factory.

3 The factory processes the carrots and puts some into bags.

4 You can buy a bag of carrots, cut them into sticks, and chow down!

CRANBERRY JUICE

1 Cranberries grow on small bushes.

2 Farmers harvest the berries, usually by flooding their fields.

3 A machine suctions the berries from the water into a truck. Then, they're sent to a factory.

4 The factory crushes the berries into juice. Yum!

OLIVE OIL

1 Olive trees grow in big groves.

2 Individual olives are picked from the trees, by hand or machine.

3 Then, the olives are crushed into liquid oil.

4 The olive oil is bottled and shipped to stores.

STRING CHEESE

1 Cows are milked, either by hand or machine.

2 Cheese makers and scientists oversee the curdling process.

3 The cheese is formed into strings at a factory.

4 The string cheese is packaged and sent on its way!

CHICKEN PATTY

1 Chickens are raised on farms, often in tight quarters.

2 The chickens are killed and their feathers removed.

3 The chicken meat is ground up with special machines.

4 The ground-up chicken is formed into patties for chicken burgers.

Exercise

Often, regular transportation is exercise!

Be Physically Active Every Day. When you eat more calories than you use, you might gain weight—so it's important to be active every day. The good news? There are tons of fun ways to exercise! What's your favorite way to play?

On the Ball! Soccer requires a lot of running around—which makes it great exercise!

SPORTY! Baseball is great exercise, too. And what about swimming, running, rollerblading, frisbee, or hula-hooping?

HOW MANY CALORIES AM I BURNING?

This box shows how many calories a 70-pound person uses during one hour of several common activities. Generally, the more your heart races, the more calories you're burning. It's no wonder jumping jacks are better for you than watching TV.

RUNNING
260 calories

WATCHING TV
33 calories

SWIMMING
200 calories

SLEEPING
30 calories

Burn More, Eat More
Remember, exercise burns up calories. So the more you run around, the more food your body needs!

EASY EXERCISE

Not all exercise requires extra effort. There are many ways to get exercise without even thinking about it!

Walking, running around at recess, and climbing stairs are all examples.

You might also ask your parents to park the car farther from where you're going, walk around while on the phone, or go outside and throw a ball at recess instead of playing video games or sitting with friends.

Can you think of other ideas? These small decisions can lead to big results!

Your Pyramid!

What's Advice without Action? Now that you know all about healthy eating and exercise, the rest is up to you. Making lifestyle changes can seem really hard, but consider these tips and you'll soon be stronger, have more energy, and feel better than ever before!

WEB LINK

The USDA's site has lots of games and info.

www.mypyramid.gov/kids/index.html

EAT RIGHT   EXERCISE   HAVE FUN!

Now that you've mastered the Pyramid, how will you stay healthy?

Make Choices That Are Right For You
Everyone has their own path to good health. Talk to your friends and family about their choices, and check out the USDA Web site for more tips.

Take One Step at a Time
You don't need to change overnight. Try starting with one new, good habit, and add one more every week.

It's All About You!
Making balanced choices will help you live longer and stay happier. The better fed your body, the better YOU you'll be!

Glossary

artery a muscular tube that carries blood from your heart to your organs and tissue

boil cooking food in a bath of boiling water

calories measure how much energy your body gets from a certain food. Calories come from carbohydates, fat, and protein.

carbohydrates come from most food groups, and are an important source of calories.

deep fry cooking food in a bath of hot oil

fat is a concentrated source of energy. It's important for cell structure and helps your body absorb some vitamins.

fiber plant structures that help your digestive tract work properly

protein makes up most of your body tissue and helps your body grow and repair

roast cooking uncovered food in a very hot oven or next to a heat source

sauté cooking in a pan with a small amount of fat

sodium is the mineral that makes up salt. Too much sodium can contribute to high blood pressure.

steam using the steam from a boiling water to cook food

vitamins and minerals are substances your body needs to function. Each one has a certain purpose. For example, *Vitamin C* helps your immune system, and *calcium* helps your bones stay strong.

So long and stay healthy!

Acknowledgments

A big Pyramid-Pete shout out to Meira Held, a truly fabulous intern, researcher, and thinker. Special thanks to Lisa Young for her nutrition expertise (for further information, visit her Web site at www.portionteller.com). Thanks to Karen Shooter for her transatlantic patience, Callum Anderson for modeling, and to Bill Miller and John Searcy for their pyramid-polishing heroics!